SECRETS FOR
The Beautiful Life

THE BEAUTIFUL LIFE IS YOURS
DISCOVER HOW

COSMAS INYANG GLOBAL VOICE, TRANSFORMING NATIONS

Note that the information in this book is inspirational and does not substitute for treatment or professional help.

ISBN. 978-978-968-797-8 Secrets for the beautiful life

Published by Beautiful Communications
For publishing partnerships, sales partnerships, sales orders, inquiries or to contact the Author

Please Contact Beautiful Communications
Email: beautifulcommunications@gmail.com
Phone: +2349072023775

Beautiful Communications
Lekki, Lagos, Nigeria

TABLE OF Content

Acknowledgments

CHAPTER 1
The Beautiful Life

CHAPTER 2
Your Identity

CHAPTER 3
Discover You

CHAPTER 4
**Forget the Past,
Break Free**

CHAPTER 5
**Be Clear About
What You Want**

CHAPTER 6
**Pray, Believe
and Receive**

CHAPTER 7
**The Principle
of Asking**

CHAPTER 8
**Your Expectations
and Your Actions**

CHAPTER 9
Take Action

CHAPTER 10
**The Power of
Focus**

CHAPTER 11
Imagine It

CHAPTER 12
**Write Down
Your Goals**

CHAPTER 13
**The Power of Prayer
and Scripture
Reading**

CHAPTER 14
**The Power of
Meditation**

CHAPTER 15
**The Power of
Declaration**

CHAPTER 16
**Your Mind
and You**

CHAPTER 17
**Your Thoughts
and You**

CHAPTER 18
Renew Your Mind

CHAPTER 19
**Your Mind and
Your Health**

CHAPTER 20
Grace for Riches

CHAPTER 21
**The Seed of
Relationships**

CHAPTER 22
**Your Feelings
and You**

CHAPTER 23
**The Power of
Supernatural Joy**

CHAPTER 24
**The Love
Command**

CHAPTER 25
**Check the Way
You See**

CHAPTER 26
**Overcoming the
Unwanted**

CHAPTER 27
Creative Thinking

CHAPTER 28
**The Power of
Routine**

CHAPTER 29
**The Power of
Practice**

CHAPTER 30
**Increase Your
Consciousness**

CHAPTER 31
Keep Upgrading

CHAPTER 32
Be Grateful

CHAPTER 33
The Power of Rest

CHAPTER 34
The Ultimate

CHAPTER 35
Be Awakened

**Affirmation
for Salvation**

Dedication

This book is dedicated to
The Lord Jesus Christ.

Acknowledgment

My special thanks and my
deepest appreciation goes to
The Almighty God

Through skillful and Godly
Wisdom is a house, a life, a
home, a family built, and by
Understanding it is established
on a sound and good foundation,

And by Knowledge shall it's
chambers be filled with all
precious and pleasant riches.

PROVERBS 24:3-4
(AMPLIFIED VERSION)

The Beautiful Life

God's plan and provision for us, is for us to have and enjoy life, and to have it in abundance.

We are to have and enjoy this life to the full, till it overflows.

God has given us everything, He has given us all.

All that we have to do is to be awakened to this knowledge, because it is when we are awakened to this knowledge and we walk in the light of this knowledge, that we begin to fully experience and enjoy the reality of all that God has done and provided for us.

You can have all that you want to have and you can be all that you want to be,

You can live and enjoy what ever quality and standard of life that you want, dream or ever imagine.

The life that God has provided for us is the abundant life, the overflowing life, the sweet life, the lavish life, The Good Life and yet the purposeful life.
I call this life, The Beautiful Life.

To briefly understand why I call this kind of life The Beautiful Life is to imagine The Beauty and Love of God visibly and physically manifesting in all aspects of your life in a way that is far beyond any degree that you can ever imagine or desire.

This kind of life is wholesome, which means that you are greatly blessed in all things,

you are greatly blessed with all things and you are greatly blessed in all aspects of your life.

Nothing lacking, Nothing Missing.

Nothing lacking, Nothing Missing.

Also be awakened to this truth that you are born to live and enjoy the beautiful life now and always, and that every kind of favor and every kind of earthly blessing is designed and ordered to always rush to you in abundance, in order to make you self sufficient at all times, no matter the case or circumstances.

Be awakened to the truth that with the beautiful life that God has given us, you are born and anointed to manifest and enjoy the blessings, favor, grace and love of God to the point that you always posses and live in the overflow such that at all times you require no help or support for anything that you want to do. This is God's plan and already settled provision for you.

The thief cometh not, but for to steal, and to kill and to destroy: I am come that they might have life, and that they might have it more abundantly.

John 10:10

Your Identity

Your basic and most important identity is that you are a child of God,

Let this regulate the way you think, talk, act, relate, your choices, decisions and everything about you.

You are Gods Greatly Beloved Child.
You are the earthly and physical reflection of God.

You are the earthly and physical expression of the image of God.

You are the expression of God's Glory and Beauty.

You can live and enjoy what ever quality and standard of life that you want, dream or ever imagine.

Everything gives birth to it's kind,

A Lion gives birth to a lion and The child of a lion is a lion,

This means that as a child of God, you are a god.

You are a God being.

As a child of God you have the life and nature of God.

You are a God being, you are Supernatural and Your body is the Temple of The Holy Spirit.

Love is your nature because God is love.

You are indestructible, You are incorruptible, You are eternal, You are Super Blessed,

You are The Righteousness of God in Christ Jesus.

You are The Righteousness of God in Christ Jesus.

As a child of God, You are from above, you are a citizen of Heaven and everything about you is Heavenly.

Always be conscious that you are Heavenly and You are only in the earth at this time for a purpose.

Live and function on earth like a diplomat, a Heavenly Diplomat.

Wherever you are dwelling here on earth becomes Heaven's embassy and an extension of Heaven.

The Provision, Protection, Security, Operations, Instructions and Standards of a Diplomat in a particular country comes from the Headquarter country that sent him or her.

You are Heavens Diplomat on Earth and you are the responsibility of The Government of Heaven.

Your Provision, Protection, Operations, Instructions, Standards and everything comes from Heaven.

But as many as received Him, to them gave He power to become the sons of God, even to them that believe on His Name:

Which were born not of blood, nor of the will of the flesh, nor of the will of man but of God.

John 1:12-13

Discover You

Every change begins with a realization,

It is when you know YOU that you can function well,

It is when you know who you are and what you've got, that you can maximize your gifts and fulfill your purpose.

To fully know who you are, you have to Study you, Discover you and Get to Know all the Beautiful things about you.

When you fully know who you are, you will begin to value you more and love you more,

To love and value you is to appreciate and be grateful to God because you are Gods idea,

You are Gods vision.

And because you are Gods idea, you are a great success,

You are more than any machine that will ever be invented by man.

You are more intelligent and efficient than any computer device that will ever be invented by man.

You are more than any animal or thing,

You are God's best.

You are God's best.

When you fully know who you are, you will
stop comparing yourself to an animal or a
man made machine or anything,

You are Gods masterpiece,

You are Gods best,

Get to discover your abilities,

There is no weakness in you because there is
no weakness in God.

Any expression of weakness is learnt, copied
or allowed consciously or unconsciously.

Any expression of weakness is foreign,

And it can be discarded and should be
discarded.

You are excellent, you are limitless.

That the communication of thy faith may become effectual by the acknowledging of every good thing which is in you in Christ Jesus.

Philemon 1:6

Forget the Past, Break Free

To embrace and enjoy the new, you have to forget the misfortunes and the disappointments of the past, because when one focuses on the negative past, the difficult past and the unpleasant past, he or she may get more negative things, more difficult things and more unpleasant things in the future.

Playing back the past, for the purpose of learning from previous mistakes is okay, but don't dwell on them for so long.

Break free from the unwanted, Break free from the limitations, and step into a new world of possibilities.

Break free from inherited patterns, Break free from cultural and societal dictates,

Break free from negative repetitions and cycles, Break free from darkness,

Break free from whatever kept you bound, for your future starts now.

You have been set free by The Lord Jesus Christ already but it is your responsibility to Stand up and walk out from whatever used to keep you bound. It starts from your mind.

Walk out of whatever you have been set free from, To walk out is your responsibility.

Let go, of the unpleasant past, Begin to set new goals for your beautiful future.

Intentionally set your mind only on the beautiful things that you want.

Know, that no matter how beautiful the past was, your future is always more beautiful because you are a child of God.

Think New and Beautiful thoughts,

Expect The New, Expect The more Beautiful.

Expect The New

Forgive anyone that hurt or offended you in
the past,

Love God, Love yourself and Love people.
Be happy and Have Faith,

Trust God, Trust His words and take steps,

Your future is so bright and so beautiful and
The beautiful life is yours, live it and enjoy it.

Do not earnestly remember the former things; neither consider the things of old.

Behold I am doing a new thing! Now it springs forth; do you not perceive and know it and will you not give heed to it?

I will even make a way in the wilderness and rivers in the desert.

Isaiah 43:18-19

Be Clear About What You Want

All things are yours but for you to receive and enjoy what you desire and ask, you have to be clear about what you want.

The clarity and decisiveness of what you really want is very important because this will open you up to receive from God.

In life, when you know what you want, this will determine what you ask for, The doors you Knock and where you go.

When you are not clear about what you want, you are wavering or double minded and The Scriptures says that anyone that asks wavering or that asks with a double mind will not receive from God.

When a person doesn't know what he or she really wants, such a person is unstable and uncertain in his or her thoughts, feelings and decisions,

And this causes such a person to be unstable in all his ways or her ways.

What Specifically do you want God to do for you?

What Specifically do you want in life? What Specifically do you want?

Knowing what you really want is the beginning of receiving,

Knowing what you really want, guides what you accept.

Knowing what you really want, guides your decisions, actions and pursuits.

Be decisive, clear, detailed and specific about what you want.

Be decisive, clear, detailed and specific

When you know what you want and have
decided on what you want,

You have to forget about the things you
don't want and just switch your thoughts,
desires, expectations, actions and focus to
what you now want.

When the solution comes, the problem goes
away.

When light comes, darkness goes away.

But let him ask in faith, nothing wavering. For he that wavereth is like the wave of the sea driven with the wind and tossed.

For let not that man think that he shall receive anything of The Lord.

A double minded man is unstable in all his ways.

James 1:6-8

Pray, Believe and Receive

He that Believes, Receives.

All things whatsoever you shall ask in prayer, when you ask believing, you shall receive.

And after you have asked The Lord in Prayer, the next thing is to believe that you have received.

What things so ever you desire or really want, when you pray, believe that you have received, then you shall receive.

After asking The Lord in Prayer, see what you want as already yours.

You must keep an attitude of joy and Thanksgiving knowing that it's already yours.

Never be bothered about how it is going to happen or how it is going to come,

Just have Faith in God.

Rest and let your heart be full of joy.

Let your heart be full of joy.

When you say, you believe, you should Think, Feel, Talk and Act that way.

All things are possible to the one that believes.

You are a child of God and the whole of creation is waiting for your manifestation,

To fully manifest and be transformed you have to renew your mind with The Word of God,

Your mind is where it all begins.

And all things, whatsoever ye shall ask in prayer, believing, ye shall receive.

Mathew 21:22

The Principle of Asking

The Principle of "Asking" was established by The Lord Jesus in the scriptures when He said:

Ask and it shall be given you

For everyone that asketh receiveth

It is important for you to note that this principle is not just a principle for prayer but a principle for life.

When you don't understand or you want something, asking opens you up to the solution and a new world of possibilities and opportunities.

Sometimes people receive not, because they ask not.

**After you have decided what you really want,
the next step is for you to ask The Lord in
prayer.**

**And when you go to The Lord in Prayers
to ask, it is important that you do so with
boldness and the assurance to receive.**

Ask knowing that God is your Father and that
He loves you so much,

Ask knowing that you are a heir of The Kingdom
of God,

Ask knowing that all things are yours and
already available, waiting for you to receive and
enjoy them,

Ask knowing that with God all things are
possible.

With God, all things are possible.

When you ask The Lord for anything in prayer, you must ask knowing that He has heard you and because he has heard you, Trust that it is settled.

And because you know it is settled, you don't have to ask again but you just keep thanking God.

Believe that you have received the very moment you asked,

And when you believe that you have received, you shall see the manifestations of that which you asked.

The Principle of Asking

Ask and it shall be given you; Seek, and ye shall find; Knock, and it shall be opened unto you:

For everyone that asketh receiveth; and he that seeketh findeth;

And to him that knocketh it shall be opened.

Mathew 7:7-8

Your Expectations and Your Actions

Expectation is a strong feeling that something good is about to happen to you,

It is a strong feeling that your prayers, your desires and that which you want is about to manifest.

Expectation is a powerful force that pulls that which you are expecting to you.

What are you looking out to see? What are you looking forward to?

What are you hoping to hear? What are you thinking will happen to you soon?

Always expect good thing to come to you always,

Always expect good things to happen to you always,

Never expect anything bad or negative.

Let your expectations be based on The Word of God, for your expectations shall not be cut off.

Always think that something sweet and beautiful is about to happen to you.

Always Expect to hear good news about your life and others.

Let your actions align with your expectations. Prepare for the good or the beautiful changes that you are expecting.

Make room for the good or the beautiful change that you are expecting.

Plan, Prepare and Take Actions concerning that which you are expecting.

Your actions should never contradict your expectations.

Never contradict your expectations.

It is important that you act and take steps
in the direction of your purpose, dreams,
visions and expectations.

Act as if you are receiving that which you are
expecting.

Your actions should always align with your
trust in God and His word.

Let your actions always align with what is
good for God and humanity.

For surely there is an end; and thine expectations shall not be cut off.

Proverbs 23:18

Take Action

Take steps towards achieving your goals, vision, dreams or ideas.

You may not have the full picture of how to accomplish your goals, vision, dreams or ideas, but as you take the first step or make the first move the next phase in it's beauty and possibilities will unfold unto you.

It may look uncertain, impossible and challenging but as you take the first step in faith, you will see a world of success, possibilities and opportunities opening up to you.

Whatever it is that you want to do, Just start, take the first step, make the first move, for with God All things are possible.

Stop complaining about what you don't have to start with,

Start with what you have, All that you need to start, is all that you have now.

What you have now is enough to start,

Change your perspective and begin to look inward and look around you to see what you have.

When people fall from a former accomplished position or they have lost what they had,

Sometimes they find it difficult to start again,

In such a situation, one should stop worrying about the past but should look inward for the remnant and start again with the remnant.

There is always a remnant and if there is no remnant, God will send you a seed.

God will send you a seed.

All things are possible to him that believes,

Believe you can, know that you can, declare that you can and act like you can.

The change begins when you think you can.

Take the first step and you will be amazed at the successful outcome of each phase.

You can do all things through the strength of The Lord that is at work in you.

You can achieve anything, You can do anything, You are Unlimited,

You are Blessed and whatever you do prospers.

And Jesus looking upon them saith, with men it is impossible, but not with God:

For with God all things are possible.

Mark 10:27

The Power of Focus

To focus is to give full attention or to concentrate your energy, thoughts, time and other resources on your goals, vision, dream, idea, task or project.

Focus more on what you want.

What you focus on, you become.

What you focus on, you accomplish.

What you focus on, grows.

What you focus on, expands.

Focus intelligently.

Focus strategically.

Focus with a target.

Focus wisely.

Focus requires discipline.

Focus intentionally.

What you concentrate your thoughts on, is likely to manifest.

What you give attention to will expand.

Let your success be your focus,

Let God be your focus.

Let God be your focus.

It's in you, Focus on cultivating that which
you have on the inside.

When that which is inside is cultivated, the
harvest will appear on the outside.

When you start focusing on what you want,
what you don't want will disappear.

When Light emerges, darkness disappears.

When you start focusing on higher, bigger
and better things, the smaller ones are
settled,

Because the lesser is in the higher.

Let your eyes look right on with fixed purpose,

and let your gaze be straight before you.

Proverbs 4:25

(Amplified Version)

Imagine It

**To imagine is to create
a mental image of
an idea, solution,
desire, expectations or
possibilities.**

Your imagination is your creative ability, When you are imagining, you are creating. Control your mind to imagine beautiful things only.

Make it a habit to read specific promises of God unto you in the Scriptures and begin to imagine beautiful things about your life based on that particular Scriptures.

What do you want? Imagine YOU receiving it, possessing it and enjoying it.

Imagine the accomplishment of your written goals.

Imagine YOU living and enjoying perfect health.

Imagine YOU living and enjoying abundance.

Imagine who you want to be.

Imagine who you want to be.

Imagine the kind of life you want to live and enjoy.

Imagine your beautiful relationship.

Imagine your prosperous business and career.

Imagine YOU living and enjoying the beautiful life.

Imagine YOU enjoying the Goodness of The Lord.

The good news is that God will do for you super-abundantly far over and above your imagination.

And The Lord said, Behold they are one people and they have all one language;

And this is only the beginning of what they will do, and now nothing they have imagined they can do will be impossible for them.

Genesis 11:6

(Amplified Version)

Write Down Your Goals and Visions

Writing down your goals, visions or ideas is part of the creative process.

It should be simple, clear and easy to understand.

In the Scriptures, The Lord instructed Prophet Habakuk to write down the vision and make it plain upon tablets, that everyone who passes may be able to read it easily and quickly as he hastens by.

This scriptural instruction, apart from revealing a Principle, has also given us deeper insights about the art of writing and the benefits by stating that the writing should be plain;

This means that it should be simple, clear, bold, short and easy to understand.

Writing down your goals, vision and ideas helps you to pursue and accomplish them.

Writing helps you remember your thoughts.

Writing guides your focus,

Writing helps you refine your thoughts.

Writing stimulates new ideas and strategies.

What you write you believe,

What you write you are persuaded,

And what you believe and what you are persuaded, you will pursue.

What you believe, you will pursue.

Apart from writing down your vision, goals and ideas, it is also very important to note that when writing to communicate with others, it should be short, clear and easy to understand, as this will bring about quick and prompt action, reaction, feedback or response from the reader, depending on the intent of the write up.

And The Lord answered me and said, Write the vision and engrave it so plainly upon tablets that everyone who passes may be able to read it easily and quickly as he hastens by.

Habakuk 2:2

(Amplified Version)

The Power of Prayers and Scripture Reading

When you pray God hears you and because He loves you and He hears you, the answers are sure.

Your prayer is powerful and produces wonderful results.

Know that Prayer is not just a communication between you and God or a time to make request,

It is also an act of worship.

Prayer time is a spiritual time of meeting or fellowship between you and God.

The more you pray, The more you are awakened to the love of God and to His Fatherhood.

In addition to prayers, reading the Scriptures is very important.

The Scriptures is The Word of God and Carries the energy of God.

Practice reading the scriptures aloud everyday,

As you do this, fresh positive energy will be released into you.

Reading aloud the scriptures will cleanse your mind, refresh you, heal you, boost your health and transform you.

The Word of God is Powerful and Quick to bring about manifestations,

Practice reading aloud Specific Scriptures that talks about the areas of your desires or expectations,

As you do this, the quick manifesting Power of the Scriptures will release faith into you and also bring about a manifestation of your desires and expectations.

Practice reading the scriptures

Just like food to your body, daily reading
and meditation on the Scriptures is very
important for daily living.

The Lord Jesus revealed this in the scriptures
when He said:

Man shall not live and be upheld and be
sustained by bread alone, but by every word
that comes forth from The Mouth of God.

If ye abide in me, and my words abide in you,

Ye shall ask what ye will, and it shall be done unto you.

John 15:7

The Power of Meditation

Meditation is dwelling on a particular thought and making declarations about that thought until you have or see the physical manifestation and success of that thought.

Meditation is very important because in the scriptures, The Almighty God instructed Joshua to Meditate, in order for him to prosper in his ways, have good success and in the fulfillment of his purpose which was to take territories.

And so in the fulfillment of purpose you've got to understand that Meditation is very important and that it was recommended by The Almighty God Himself.

It is very important that you dwell always on Beautiful thoughts and make Beautiful, and personalized declarations about that thought.

The source and the pillar of your meditation should always be The Word of God.

To follow the meditation pattern given to Joshua by The Lord, It is important to pay attention to the details for the lessons and principles in that instruction.

For example, It is stated in that verse to Joshua that The Word of God should not depart from his mouth.

This means that the mouth is an important place and instrument for meditation, this also means that one is to mutter, chant or make heart felt declarations with the mouth during meditation.

Another point from that verse of the scripture to Joshua is that he should meditate on The Word of God day and night. This shows us that meditation is to be done day and night.

Meditate on The Word of God

The Instruction of The Lord to Joshua
to Meditate also stated the benefits as
quoted below:

*"That you may observe and do according
to all that is written in it.
For then you shall make your way
prosperous and then you shall deal wisely
and have good success"*

The above quote from the instruction
verse to Joshua, shows us that, as you
meditate, you shall receive Strategies,
Instructions, Insights, Revelations, Ideas,
Knowledge, Know how, Supernatural
information, illuminations, Enlightenments
and Awakenings.

Meditation will also cause you to take
wise actions based on the Supernatural
Information or revelation that you have
received during Meditation.
Meditation will cause you to deal wisely,
this means that you will function with
Supernatural Wisdom,

Meditation leads to Transformation and
also releases and activates supernatural
wisdom in you,

And then you shall make your way
prosperous and have good success.

This book of the law shall not depart out of thy mouth; but thou shall meditate therein day and night, that thou mayest observe to do according to all that is written therein: for then thou shall make thy way prosperous, and then thou shall have good success.

Joshua 1:8

The Power of Declaration

Declaration simply means speaking out with your mouth.

Declaration or Confession is also responding and speaking in alignment or in agreement with The Word of God.

It also means believing and speaking out with your mouth what The Word of God says concerning you and His promises for you.

Declaration is a principle and an act that releases power to create, power to recreate, power to direct, power to redirect, power to receive, power to activate and the list goes on.

**Declaration has to come from the heart
because an effective and powerful declaration
is that which proceeds from strong belief,
understanding and mixed with positive
emotions.**

**If you believe in your heart and declare with
your mouth, you shall have what you say,**

For with the heart you believe and with your
mouth you Declare it into manifestation.

When you accept, believe and declare the Word
of God, you are responding and speaking in
alignment with God and when you speak in
response and alignment with The Word of God,
manifestations is sure.

Believing, Personalizing and Declaring with
your mouth a particular Scripture, brings into
physical manifestation that which that Scripture
talks about..

When you make declarations, believe that, that
declaration shall surely come to pass.

When you make declarations, believe

Your tongue is like the compass of a ship and the compass of a ship is a tool used to steer the ship in the direction that it should go.

So you can use the power of your tongue to steer your life in the direction of your desire or choice through your regular and consistent declaration.

Creation was spoken into existence and manifestation by God.

What really do you want? Speak it into manifestation.

Conceive it, Imagine it, believe it, write it down and keep declaring it until you have it.

What you believe in your heart and declare with your mouth, will manifest.

Death and life lies in the power of the tongue, Watch what you say, for there is power in your words.

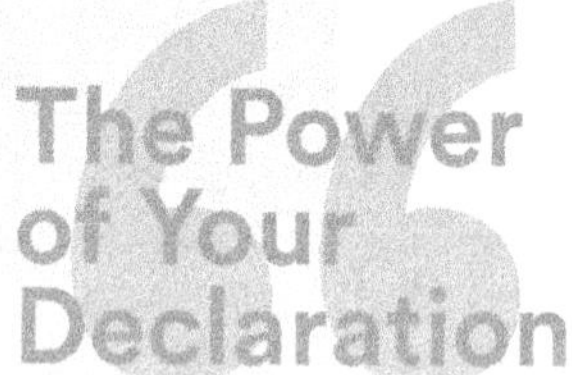

Death and life are in the power of the tongue:

And they that love it shall eat the fruit thereof.

Proverbs 18:21

Your Mind and You

Your mind is a very important part of you.

Guard your mind with all diligence because the issues of life and everything you do, flows from your mind.

When you take charge of your mind, you take charge of your thoughts and when you take charge of your thoughts, you take charge of your life.

Take charge of your mind by controlling your thoughts, what you see, what you listen to, and what you read.

The mind is like a garden and whatever you plant or allow inside your mind will grow.

What you allow into your mind, think, feel and dwell on for a long period of time, will reflect or manifest in your life.

The mind is also like a battle field and every victory is first achieved in the mind.

No matter what happens around you, never lose the battle in your mind.

Win it first in your mind,

Achieve it first in your mind,

See it first in your mind,

Receive it first in your mind.

Your mind pulls and your mind repels.

Receive it first in your mind.

Your life to a large extent is regulated by your thoughts, and this takes place in your mind.

Your mind regulates your speech, Your mind regulates your health, Your mind regulates your prosperity.

For you to prosper greatly in all aspects of your life and enjoy The Beautiful Life according to God's plan for you, you have to renew your mind with The Word of God.

Your life is as prosperous as your mind. Invest in your mind and Guard your mind above all that you guard.

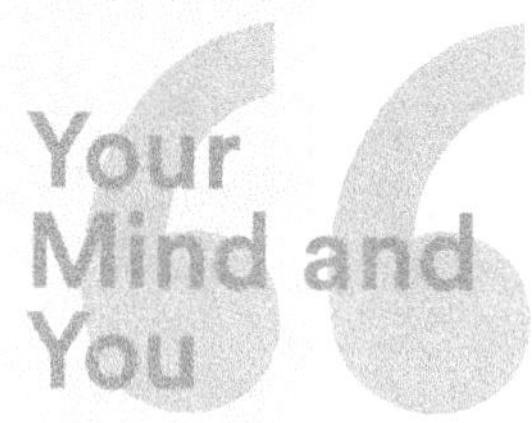

Keep and guard your heart with all vigilance and above all that you guard,

For out of it flow the springs of life.

Proverbs 4:23

(Amplified Version)

Your Thoughts And You

As a man thinks in his heart, so is he.

Every thought is an active and creative force which will manifest with time and in no time,

And the kind of manifestation that you see depends on the kind of thoughts that you think.

The manifestation of a thought also depends on how intense and how long one dwells on the thought.

What you majorly think about and what you completely focus your heart on, over a period of time will manifest.

**When you have conceived a vision or
an idea, dwell completely on thoughts
of the manifestation and success of that
vision or idea, and you will surely see the
materialization and success of that vision or
idea.**

You are transformed over time and in no
time, into what you consistently, dominantly,
emotionally and deeply dwell your thoughts on,
over a period of time.

You are what you think and you become what
you think,

You become
what you think

Avoid thoughts of fear because over a
period of time, things that are consistent
with fear may manifest.

Positive thoughts will produce positive
results and negative thoughts will produce
negative results.

Let Thoughts of The Word of God,
Thoughts of Positivity, Thoughts of
Possibilities and Thoughts of Abundance,
dwell richly in your heart,

For out of your heart, out of within you,
springs forth the aspects of your life.
You create with your thoughts and with
your words.

And out of the abundance of the heart,
you think and speak forth to create your
world.

For as he thinketh in his heart, so is he:

Eat and drink, saith he to thee; but his heart is not with thee.

Proverbs 23:7

Renew Your Mind

To renew your mind is to feed, expose, awaken, enlighten and illuminate your mind with fresh, positive and higher thoughts which in turn will cause the old mindset to fall off and cause a fresh mindset to be restored.

To renew your mind, you also have to stop believing in the old thinking and to stop subscribing to the source or the information that produced the old thinking.

Be careful what you hear because fear and unbelief comes by hearing and hearing just like faith comes by hearing and hearing.

Also note that You become what you visualize or imagine over time and You Have what you think and declare over time.

Do not adapt to the negative experiences, the negative norms and traditions but arise, shine and live your life to the fullest by renewing your mind with The Word of God.

Do not be conformed to this world and to the systems of this world but be transformed by the renewing of your mind with The Word of God.

Do not be conformed to the old, the regular and the unpleasant but renew your mind with The Word of God to enjoy The New and Beautiful things that God has done for you.

When you renew your mind, you have new thinking,

And when you have new thinking you have new possibilities, new experiences and new living.

Renewing your mind gives you new focus even as it is also to focus on something new.

Renewing your mind leads to transformation and you renew your mind by meditation.

Renew your mind by meditation.

Renew your mind with thoughts of
possibilities knowing that with God All
things are possible.

Renew your mind with thoughts of
abundance knowing that you are a heir
and All things are yours.

Renew your mind with thoughts of perfect
health knowing that as The Lord Jesus is,
so are you.

Renew your mind with thoughts of
Beautiful relationships knowing that God's
plan for you is Good.

The process of renewing one's mind and
being transformed should be continuous
because there is always more, there is
always something higher and there is
always something better for you.

And be not conformed to this world: but be ye transformed by the renewing of your mind,

That ye may prove what is that good, and acceptable, and perfect, will of God.

Romans 12:2

Your Mind and Your Health

It is important for you to know that your thoughts can affect your health and wellbeing.

Negative thoughts puts stress on the body and stress is a major cause of most diseases.

Practice staying in Love always, let your heart be filled with Love for God and Love for people.

Avoid worry and stay grateful all the time,

Worry puts stress on the body.

When one is sick and is trying to get well or healed, it is important that he or she does the following: Should focus on thoughts of perfect health and also maintain an attitude of Love and Gratitude to God knowing that his or her healing has already been settled by The Lord Jesus.

Engage in what will make the person laugh and stay happy always, because Laughter is a medicine.

Practice meditating on the Scriptures that talks about God's promises concerning health and healing.

Talk less about the disease and present symptoms but talk more about complete recovery and perfect health.

Avoid the thoughts and fear of disease or sickness,

Avoid hearing or talking sickness so that the fear of sickness will not get into you.

Avoid negative habits and attitude that is not good for the body,

know that your body is a temple of The Holy Spirit and that you have a responsibility to take care of your body. Avoid stress and routinely engage in Rest and Relaxation.

Rest and Relax.

Fill your heart with positive thoughts and
positive feelings all the time.

Let Love, Gratitude, Laughter, Happiness
and other positive habits, be your life
style.

Take The Word of God everyday like food
and medicine and declare health over your
body everyday.

As a child of God you are not supposed
to be sick or infected by any disease
because you are born of the incorruptible
seed of God and this makes you and your
body incorruptible.

The Lord Jesus is always in perfect health
and as The Lord Jesus is, so are you in this
world now.

A happy heart is good medicine and a cheerful mind works healing,

But a broken spirit dries up the bones.

Proverbs 17:22

(Amplified Version)

Grace for Riches

Riches and The Beautiful Life is your right as a child of God and yours to have and enjoy now and always.

The Lord is the source and the Giver of all good things including extreme riches.

The ideas, ability, wisdom, knowledge, capacity, opportunities and Grace for us to receive and enjoy riches, comes from The Lord.

As a child of God you are a citizen of The Kingdom of God and a heir of the riches of the Kingdom.

Through The Blessing of The Lord and The Grace of The Lord Jesus Christ you can now receive and enjoy extreme riches.

No matter where you are at the moment financially, you can change your level and get more by setting a new desired financial goal, asking The Lord in prayer, and taking inspired steps.

After asking in prayer, believe that you have received, Declare that you have received,

And then with Joy and Gratitude expect the physical manifestation, knowing it is settled and it's yours already.

Don't be concerned about how it will manifest, listen inward, for an idea and a strategy from The Holy Spirit. Also note that The Lord can also do it for you miraculously or any other way.

Always be conscious that The Lord is moving people, circumstances and events to supply to you Riches and the Good things of life in a way that surpasses your desire, want or request.

Expect the physical manifestation

To receive Riches and to increase in Riches,
you have to renew your mind with The
Scriptures concerning the promises of God
to you for Riches, Abundance and The
Beautiful life.

Always know this: that as a child of God, you
are very rich already.
You have to see yourself as already being
very Rich and think as already being very
Rich

To receive, enjoy and stay in Riches, you have
to think Abundance and think that Riches is
yours always.

Never talk or focus on lack, Focus on
overflow because The Lord has anointed you
for Abundance.

Always Think , Talk and Rejoice like you
already have it because All things are yours
already.

Never focus on bills, Focus on Abundant
Money and abundant Provision from The
Lord always.

Refuse Negative thoughts and feelings of
lack but fill your heart with the thoughts and
the Joy that you are born and blessed to live
in abundance Now and Always.

for ye know The Grace of our Lord Jesus Christ, that, though He was rich, yet for your sakes He became poor, that ye through His poverty might be rich.

2 Corinthians 8:9

The Seed of Relationships

It is God's plan for you to have beautiful and peaceful relationships.

To receive love, it is important that you think thoughts of love towards others,

As you think thoughts of love towards people, you will begin to act in love towards people, and naturally you will reap the harvest of love from people.

It's easy for love to flow out of you because God is love and you are a child of love.

The love of God has been poured out in your heart by The Holy Spirit.
If you are single and desire to have a spouse,

Pray to God about it, and after your prayer, relax and know that it is settled.

And from that moment of prayer, begin to think, talk and act based on the Faith, that it is already settled.

While still expecting to get married, it is important that you avoid worry thoughts and worry talks.

Never act in desperation or under pressure, instead, Relax and joyfully prepare for the arrival of your desired spouse.

To have a loving relationship you must love and value yourself first.

Treat and take care of yourself the way you want others to think and take care of you.

To balance this, you should also love and treat others, the way you would want others to love and treat you.

Love and value yourself first.

For married people: Husbands love your
wives as Christ loves the church and as you
love your body.

Wives submit yourselves to your own
husbands as you do unto The Lord.

Wives love, respect, honor and stay
committed and faithful to your husbands.

In general, to build a great relationship and
to make any relationship work, it is important
for you to focus on the strength of the other
person or what you like about the other
person, As you do this, it will take away
complaints and feeling of dissatisfaction,
which of course destroys relationships.

The Seed of Relationships

And as you would like and desire that men would do to you, do exactly so to them.

Luke 6:31

(Amplified Version)

Your Feelings and You

A Feeling is an emotional state or reaction,

Feelings are responses to internal or external experiences.

Thoughts and Words affect our feelings.

Positive Thoughts produce Positive feelings, Negative Thoughts produce Negative feelings.

Positive feelings pull the positives, Negative feelings pull the negatives.

Positive information produces positive feelings, Negative information produces negative feelings.

The way you feel can be used to check whether your thought is positive or negative or whether what you hear or see is positive or negative.

Disconnect from anything that makes you feel negative, bad or low.

Connect and stay connected to positive people and positive things that makes you feel happy, joyful, hopeful, expectant and optimistic.

Never dwell on any negative feeling.

Maintain Positive feelings only, and feel good about yourself always.

You can boost and uplift your feelings by listening to positive music, playing back sweet memories, talking to friends or doing positive things that makes you happy.

When you switch your thoughts, you switch your feelings.

Create and dwell always in a positive and joyful environment.

Positive feelings only

Feelings is a puller of things that are
consistent with such a feeling, or that which
is declared.

No wonder the scriptures says that with
Joy will you draw water from the wells of
salvation.

Feelings can either speed up or slow down
the physical manifestations of our desires,
requests and expectations.

Negative feelings slows down or hinders
manifestations, while positive feelings speeds
up or brings about manifestations.

The feelings that you should always have,
should be the feelings of Happiness, Love
and Joy.

A merry heart doeth good like a medicine:

But a broken spirit drieth the bones.

Proverbs 17:22

The Power of Supernatural Joy

Supernatural Joy is a special kind of Joy that is planted in us by The Holy Spirit and this kind of Joy bubbles forth in us like a fountain.

The Scriptures calls this The Joy of The Lord or The Joy of The Holy Spirit.

Supernatural Joy is a fruit of The Holy Spirit.

This kind of Joy is never a momentary or temporary feeling that is induced by drugs, sex, alcohol, entertainment or companionship.

This kind of Joy is spiritual and long lasting.

The Scriptures says, with Joy shall you draw water from the wells of Salvation,

This means that With Supernatural Joy, you bring into manifestation The Blessings of God in your life.

Supernatural Joy is a catalyst and a breeding place for Miracles and The Manifestations of The Word of God and Blessings.

Supernatural Joy is Supernatural strength, this means Supernatural ability.

And through this Supernatural Strength which is Supernatural Ability, you can do all things.

No wonder The Scriptures says you can do all things through Christ that strengthens you,

This strength is released through Supernatural Joy, For The Scriptures says The Joy of The Lord is your strength.

The Joy of The Lord is your strength.

We can allow Supernatural Joy to flow through us and we can also block it or refuse to express it.

That is why The Scriptures repeatedly instructs us and reminds us to "Rejoice".

To Rejoice means to feel Joy, to show Joy or to express Joy.

This means one can choose not to show joy especially when in an unpleasant situation but it is in such a situation that we are instructed repeatedly to Rejoice because Joy is a weapon, an environment and a catalyst for Miracles.

If you have a turned OFF - torch light in your hand and darkness comes, in order to see, it is your responsibility to turn ON the torch light to show light, so like wise, it is your responsibility to acknowledge, show, express and stay in Joy.

Therefore with joy shall ye draw water out of the wells of salvation.

Isaiah 12:3

The Love Command

Love is a heart thing that reflects in our actions, our words, our attitude, our thoughts and our viewpoints.

God is Love, this means that as a child of God, you are love.

And because love is your nature, it means that you can easily and freely express love all the time.

God is Love and you are a child of love, this also means that it's in you to Love.

Your natural and default frequency should be Love because you are Love.

You are commanded by God to Love God, Love yourself and to Love people.

In the Garden of Eden, the commandment was for Adam not to eat the fruit of the tree of knowledge of good and evil.

In the old testament the Israelites were given the ten commandments.

The new commandment for the present day living as revealed and released by The Lord Jesus is for us to Love The Lord with all our heart, our soul and our strength and also love our neighbors as ourselves.

To love our neighbors is to love people.

Love God,
Love yourself,
Love people.

To walk in forgiveness is to walk in love.
You are in your purest form, when you walk
in love.

When you operate in Love, you are operating
in the most positive feeling.

Love is a powerful and positive force, when
you walk in love, you are walking in the realm
of positivity.

When you walk in love, everything works and
everything positive moves speedily towards
you.

When you walk in love, you win all the time.
You enjoy all the blessings when you walk in
love.

Walking in Love releases an empowerment
into your life that causes you to prosper.
Love makes faith effective, Walking in Love
causes your Faith to produce greater results.
Walking in love makes you enjoy the fullness
of The Blessings of God.

A new commandment I give unto you, that ye love one another as I have loved you,

That ye also love one another.

John 13:34

Check the Way You See

The way you see what you see is very important.

The way you see things affects your judgment and your judgment affects your decisions and choices.

The way you see things affects your thoughts and your words.

The way you see determines the feelings and the energy that flows through you.

The way you see determines your actions and the results that you get.

It's important that you always see things from a positive point of view only.

Always see everything from the perspective of love.

Always see everything based on your identity as a child of God and God's great love for you.

See everything based on the Lessons, Instructions, Truth, Knowledge, Wisdom and Revelation from The Scriptures and The Holy Spirit.

In the Scriptural Story of David and Goliath, the armies of Israel saw a giant that they were trying to defeat while David saw a defeated man by the power of God.

David at that time was a boy with no military experience facing a giant warrior but he didn't consider his lack of military experience or lack of personal military weapons but on The Power of The God of Israel.

While Goliath was a giant and a warrior with military trainings, experience and heavy military weapons but David paid no attention to the size of the giant, his threats, size of army or his weapons.

David saw Goliath differently, others saw a problem too big but he saw a problem too small before God,

And so with a stone and a sling, a boy who dared to see a problem differently defeated a giant warrior.

David who was a Shepherd boy later became the king of Israel and a man after God's heart.

See problems differently

Never worry about anything but in all things know that God loves you so much and that He is always with you.

No matter the situation, no matter where you are or no matter what you have done, The Almighty God will never leave you nor forsake you. You are Always Unstoppable, Indomitable and Protected.

You are God's Greatly beloved child and The Beautiful life is yours, See all things this way all the time.

While we look not at the things which are seen, but at the things which are not seen:

For the things which are seen are temporal; but the things which are not seen are eternal.

2 Corinthians 4:18

Overcoming The Unwanted

To overcome or avoid the things you don't want, all you have to do is to switch to the things you want.

Switch your thoughts from that which you don't want to what you want.

Avoid focusing on the unwanted experience because the more you focus on it, the more it expands.

The scriptures states that, at a particular point in time, when the earth was without form and an empty waste and darkness was upon the face of the very great deep, The Spirit of The Lord was moving upon the face of the waters, and God said let there be light and there was light.

From this Scriptural illustration, a principle of dealing with the unwanted was established.

Switch your thoughts

Light is the opposite of darkness,

And when darkness was upon the face of the very great deep, God called forth the very opposite of darkness, which is Light.

Note that He didn't talk about the darkness or acknowledge the darkness,

He didn't say darkness go away,

He called forth Light and Light came forth.

And when light comes, darkness disappears and darkness can never overcome light.

When abundance comes, lack disappears.

Never resist the unwanted, just switch your thoughts, emotions, prayers, words and actions to that which you want.

And the earth was without form and void; and darkness was upon the face of the deep.

And The Spirit of God moved upon the face of the waters.

And God said, let there be light and there was light.

Genesis 1:2-3

Creative Thinking

Creative Thinking is to think differently, It is thinking outside the box, it is thinking from a different, higher and possibility perspective.

It is thinking based on The Word and by the inspiration of The Holy Spirit.

You are a fountain of ideas and solutions.
Take time out to think creatively, deeply and intentionally.

Creative Thinking unlocks ideas, Creative Thinking refines ideas.

Creative Thinking makes a vision clearer, Creative Thinking births new ideas.

Creative Thinking births strategies to help you accomplish your ideas or vision.

The Scriptures says a man's heart deviseth his way: but The Lord directeth his steps.

This means that it is important to plan and good planning is done during creative thinking.

Creative Thinking helps you to deal wisely,

The Scriptures says the heart of the righteous man studieth the answer, but the heart of the wicked poureth out evil things.

Think intentionally

The Scriptures says, it is the Glory of The Lord to conceal a thing, but the honor of kings is to search out a matter.

The solution is in you, All that you have to do is to search it out through Creative Thinking.

It is The Glory of God to conceal a thing:

But the honor of Kings is to search out a matter.

Proverbs 25:2

The Power of Routine

Your routine is what you consistently do everyday and in most cases at a particular time or duration.

Success and failure is hidden in one's daily routine, This means that success and failure is hidden in what you do everyday.

Check your daily activities, if they are not productive or if they wont lead to your desired success, then it's important that you change or modify your activities.

How you start your day is very important in the outcome of that day.

And how you start your day everyday is very important in your overall success per time.

It's important that you start your day with God by starting your day with Prayers, Scripture Reading and Meditation.

Waking up to God is waking up to Love, Inspiration, Blessings and Positive and Powerful energy for the day.

Wake up to Joy, Avoid worry thoughts or negative words and emotions in the morning as you wake.

Importantly, how you end your day everyday, also determines how you start the next day.

End your day planning for the next day and speaking what you desire to see the next day.

End your day with gratitude to God for the just ended day and the blessings for the next day.

End your day with Prayers, Scripture reading, Meditation, thoughts of Love, Gratitude and Joy.

End your day with Great positive imaginations and expectations for the next day.

End your day with expectations for the next day.

Routine births habits and our habits channels
our actions in a particular way which in turn
determines the direction and to an extent
the overall outcome of one's life.

Your daily routine should be based on your
identity, your beliefs, your purpose, your
goals, your vision, your mission, your targets,
your projects, your work and perhaps your
geographical location.

Routine births cycles and patterns; If you
don't like a particular cycle or pattern or if
you want to change or improve your cycles,
then change your routine.

Every successful person has a Success
Routine, There is something he or she does
everyday that has taken and kept him or her
on top. Create your Success Routine.

And he came out and went, as was His habit, to the mount of Olives,

and the disciples also followed Him.

Luke 22:39

(Amplified Version)

The Power of Practice

It is God's plan for you to live well and enjoy The Beautiful Life.

Suffering of any kind is never God's plan for you,

Neither does God want you to enjoy in some aspects and suffer in some other aspects.

God wants you to enjoy all aspects of your life.

The Lord has given you all things that pertains to living and enjoying The Beautiful Life but It's your responsibility to Seek knowledge, Accept and Believe what you know and to Do what you know.

**The reason why some people are not living
and enjoying according to God's plan is
because they are not aware of The Beautiful
Life that God has already planned and
Prepared for them,**

**And for some people they are aware but they
don't know what to do or how to bring it into
manifestation.**

And for some people, they have the
information, but they don't believe it, so they
are not doing it,

While some know what to do, they believe it
but they are not doing it,

However it is those that know what to do,
believe it and keep doing it, that are living and
enjoying and also seeing greater results in
their lives.

The purpose of this book is to show you
some of the things that you should do to live
and enjoy The Beautiful Life but it is your
responsibility to believe them and Practice
them.

Know, believe, do.

Practice is not a one-off action, it is doing something repeatedly, persistently and consistently with a goal until you see the results or until you become.

Practice what you know and what you will get to know from reading this book.

Practice, takes you from just knowing, hearing or reading to doing, and result comes from doing,

Not just doing it once, but you have to keep doing it until you see results and it becomes a lifestyle.

You get better at what you do repeatedly, regularly and consistently.

Mastery comes with practice.
And you also see better and greater results when you do the right things persistently, regularly, repeatedly and consistently.

The Power of Practice

And if you know these things, blessed and happy and to be envied are you if you practice them,

If you act accordingly and really do them.

John 13:17

(Amplified Version)

Increase Your Consciousness

To be conscious is to be deeply awakened, alert, dominantly aware and responsive to what you have come to know, believe and fully persuaded of.

Whatever you are constantly and dominantly conscious of, you activate.

Meditation births consciousness and you can increase your consciousness in a particular aspect by increasing your meditation in that aspect.

Consciousness accelerates manifestations and births experiences and realities. What you are conscious of determines how you act, respond or react to any thing.

What you are conscious of determines what you see and how you see things.

What you are conscious of determines your wants, goals, choices and decisions,

And your choices and decisions to an extent culminates to what you experience now and in the future.

What your are conscious of, determines your association and where you go.

Let's just say that what you are conscious of, determines your daily living, the quality and standards.

You are everything to the degree of your consciousness.

For you to live and enjoy The Beautiful Life, you have to increase your consciousness of God, your consciousness of the love of God for you, your consciousness of The Lord Jesus, your consciousness of the revelations of The Word of God and His promises, your consciousness of The Holy Spirit , your consciousness of who you are, your consciousness of the kingdom of God which you are now a citizen, your consciousness of your citizenship benefits, rights and responsibilities, your consciousness of The Truth in the Scriptures, your consciousness that you are now the righteousness of God in Christ Jesus, and your consciousness of your purpose here on earth.

Increase your consciousness of God

Be more conscious of positivity than negativity, Be more conscious of good things than bad things.

Be more conscious of abundance than lack.

Be more conscious of receiving, having, and enjoying what you want than what you don't want.

Be more conscious of Angels helping and protecting you than demons.

Be more conscious of all things working together for your good, than things not working.

**My son, attend to my words;
consent and submit to my
sayings.**

**Let them not depart from
your sight; keep them in the
center of your heart.**

**For they are life to those who
find them, healing and health
to all their flesh.**

Proverbs 4:20-22

(Amplified Version)

Keep Upgrading

You are the earthly and physical expression of God.

You are the expression of God's Glory and Beauty.

You are more than what you are per time.

You are more than what you know per time.

There is always a Greater and more Beautiful "YOU" in you.

You were made to only appreciate, Never to depreciate,

Whatever is not upgraded loses relevance in future,

It may also stand a chance of extinction.

Cultivate you, refine you, build you and upgrade you.

Be the best and excellent version of you per time.

Do all with excellence and express excellence always because you are excellence, you are perfection.

Express excellence always

Everything about you is supposed to get
better per time,

Nothing is supposed to be stagnant in your
life.

You are greatly blessed to keep making
great progress only, you are greatly blessed
to keep increasing greatly only and to keep
moving forward and higher only.

Everything around you and everything that
you touch is supposed to improve.

The whole of creation has been waiting for
you to manifest, because you carry in you
the ability to bless them, replenish them and
improve them.

You are a carrier of a special kind of energy
that blesses and improves everything that
you touch or that comes in contact with you.

There is always something better, there is
always something more beautiful, it keeps
unfolding.

Never be satisfied at any level, keep
upgrading because there is always more.

But the path of the uncompromisingly just and righteous is like the light of dawn, that shines more and more, brighter and clearer until it reaches the full strength and glory in the perfect day to be prepared.

Proverbs 4:18

(Amplified Version)

Be Grateful

In the Scriptures, Gratitude is an instruction as well as an exhortation.

The story of the 10 lepers in the Scriptures is a powerful lesson, highlighting the importance and benefits of Gratitude.

In this story, 10 lepers encountered the Lord Jesus and asked for healing and The Lord Jesus gave them an instruction to go show themselves to the priest, and as they went they were healed.

When one of them saw that he was healed, with a heart of gratitude, he turned back to The Lord Jesus, thanking Him and praising Him.

And The Lord Jesus Blessed him and made him Whole.

He got more than healing, he was completely restored.

When you are grateful, you will have more.

Switch your mind from worry and negative thoughts to thoughts of how much you have been blessed.

The simplest way to express gratitude is by sincerely saying "Thank You"

Let the memories of the blessings of the Lord be in your heart more than the thoughts of what you want God to do for you.

And every time you remember The goodness of The Lord in your life, just say "Thank You".

Never take any assistance, service or favor, from people for granted, no matter how little you think it is,

Always sincerely say "Thank You".

Gratitude should be expressed from the heart, this means that when you say "Thank You" you have to mean it from your heart, it has to be sincere and heartfelt.

Practice this many times daily and gratitude will become your habit and a lifestyle.

Sincerely say "Thank You".

Be grateful for what you already have and that which you are expecting will come.

Whatever you desire, When you ask, give thanks as if you have already received it and you shall have it.

When you are grateful, more will come into your life.

Thinking and talking from a place of gratitude will bring about manifestations of your expectations. Gratitude is a multiplier and a magnet of Beautiful things.

Staying grateful generates a positive feeling within us, and the more positive you feel, the more you pull everything Beautiful into your life and the more you multiply everything good in your life.

At all times and for everything giving thanks in The Name of our Lord Jesus Christ to God The Father.

Ephesians 5:20

(Amplified Version)

The Power of Rest

We have been born into Rest.

We have been born into that which is more than the Garden of Eden experience.

We have been born into a place and a life of Rest.

Everything for us to live and enjoy The Beautiful Life has already been finished.

You have been born into a life of no toiling.

You must know that toiling is linked to the curse.

And if toiling is linked to the curse, then The Blessing that comes from the gift of Righteousness that we have received from The Lord Jesus Christ is linked to Rest and The Beautiful life.

You are blessed, this means that you are empowered and graced to succeed and enjoy all the time.

Rest is not the absence of work but the absence of toiling and painful labor without passion or purpose.

Rest is doing something from a position of relaxation, joy, passion, purpose and fulfillment.

Functioning from a position of Rest is functioning with the consciousness that you have been born into Rest and that you have been blessed and graced to do all things and to function from a place and a position of Rest.

You always have to be conscious that Rest is the place that you are, Rest is what you have Received, Rest is what you now have and Rest is the position that you should take.

You have been born into rest

Rest is connected to Peace, Joy, Abundance, Protection, Guidance, Direction, The Goodness of The Lord, Purpose, Blessings, Overflow, Supernatural Provision, Perfect Health, Purpose, fulfillment, Happiness and every other good thing you can ever think or imagine.

The Lord Jesus is the giver of Rest and it is in Him that we find Rest.

If you are not functioning in Rest, all you have to do now is to say:

Lord Jesus, I come to you now and I receive your Rest now.

Then from this moment you are to allow the consciousness of Rest to stay in your life, and you have to be continually awakened to this consciousness of Rest and you have to do all things from REST.

Come unto me, all ye that labor and are heavy laden, and I will give you rest.

Mathew 11:28

The Ultimate

The Almighty God is the ultimate source from which all beings and all things emanates.

Every other thing or being in existence, that was, that is and that will ever be, comes from The Almighty God.

The Almighty God exceeds that which can ever be comprehended or conceived.

No mind is large enough to contain The Truth and The Reality of The Almighty God and His Power.

The Almighty God cannot be compared neither can His Greatness.

No human language can fully express The Almighty God.

No one can stand in the very presence of The Almighty God.

He is God all by Himself, there was no other God, there is no other God and there shall be no other God.

He is all power even as He is beyond all powers and any power. He is beyond Power.

He is The Perfect Light, The Source and The Sustainer of all lights, even as He is beyond Light.

We try to call or express Him based on what our minds can take but the truth is, HE is more.

Put all your trust in God and love God with all your heart and strength, for our very existence is from God, Our very existence depends on God, and our very existence is sustained by God.

Out of His love we came forth and out of His love, all things are abundantly provided for us.

Put your trust in God

To be awakened to The Almighty God is to be awakened to our true and original self.

To be awakened to The Almighty God is to be awakened to Abundance and to the flow from the very source of life.

From Him we came and in Him we live move and have our being.

Without God we can do nothing and we can be nothing, and we can have nothing.

All that we have comes from God, all that we will ever have, comes from God.

All that we want, desire or expect comes from God.

I PRAY FOR YOU:
May you be awakened to The Almighty God, and May you experience His Great Love for you and His Goodness. May you walk daily in His Light and in the knowledge of His Truth. Amen

The Ultimate

I am the vine, ye are the branches: he that abideth in me, and I in him, the same bringeth forth much fruit: for without me ye can do nothing

John 15:5

SECRETS FOR The Beautiful Life

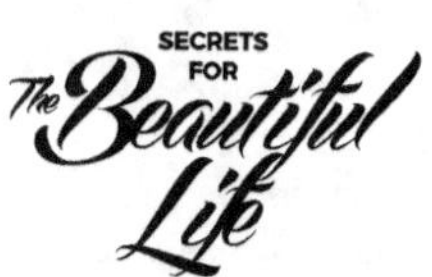

Be Awakened

Be awakened to the fatherhood of God,

Be awakened to His Great Love for you,

Be awakened to The beyond limitless, Irresistible, Indomitable and indescribable power of God,

Be awakened to His Grace and Favor at work in your life,

Be awakened to The Word of God,

Be awakened to The Lord Jesus, His Love, His Grace and His finished works for you,

Be awakened to The Power in The Blood of The Lord Jesus,

Be awakened to The Power in The Name of The Lord Jesus.

Be awakened to The Holy Spirit,

Be awakened to the presence and the ministry of The Holy Spirit in your life,

Know that The Holy Spirit is your Counselor, Helper, Advocate, Strengthener, Intercessor and Standby,

Welcome Him into your life, Acknowledge His presence in your life always, yield to Him always and do as He guides and Instructs you always.

The Holy Spirit is to you, the way The Lord Jesus was to the Apostles when He was on earth.

Welcome The Holy Spirit into your life

Be awakened to you,

Be awakened to your uniqueness, your gifts,
your strengths and your abilities,

Be awakened to your essence, your voice
and your power.

Be awakened to your purpose and your
passion.

Be awakened to your vision, your goals and
your dreams.

Be awakened to the power in your words,

Be awakened to the power of your mind,
your thoughts, your feelings and your
imagination.

Be awakened to the Glory and Blessings of
The Lord upon you and His Grace that is at
work in your life.

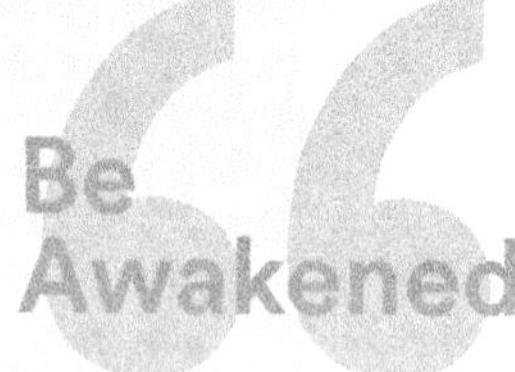

Arise, shine; for thy light has come, and The Glory of The LORD is risen upon thee.

Isaiah 60:1

Affirmation for Salvation

I believe, I agree and I declare that
The Lord Jesus Christ is The Saviour.

He came, he was crucified, He resurrected and
was Highly exalted and He is sitting now at the
right hand of The Father. His blood was shed and
is eternally active for the eternal redemption and
salvation and birth of the sons of God. * I believe,
I receive and I declare that The Lord Jesus is my
Lord and My Savior.

I receive the gift of the
righteousness of God in Christ Jesus.

I receive The Holy Spirit
and His functions in my life.

My heart believes The Word of God
and I am awakened to God always.

I am a child of God and
The Almighty God is my Father.

The Lord bless you and watch,
guard and keep you;

The Lord make His Face to shine
upon and enlighten you and be
gracious, kind, merciful, and
giving favor to you,

The Lord lift up His approving
countenance upon you and give
you peace, tranquility of heart
and life continually.

NUMBERS 6:24-26
(AMPLIFIED VERSION)